Write Your Non-Fiction Book in 4 Weeks

by Drew Becker

Book 1   Interviewing Quick Guide: The Art and Craft

Book 2   Write a Non-Fiction Book in 4 Weeks

All Rights Reserved. No part of this publication may be reproduced in any form or by any means, including scanning, photocopying, or otherwise without prior written permission of the copyright holder.
Copyright Drew Becker © 2016

ISBN-10: 1-944662-06-5

ISBN-13: 978-1-944662-06-6

Cover Art by Rockbrand Creative Jennifer Davis

Dedication

This book is dedicated to my parents who would have been pleased to see me publish another paperback book. Their support for me following my path—although none of us could see it—enabled me to become a writer. This eventuality for me was a dream for my father so I think of him each time I publish. I also want to salute my sisters for following their dreams and finding lives that are meaningful and beneficial to those around them.

Table of Contents

A Little about Me 1

Introduction 5

One-Minute Vision 9

Four-Minute Foundations 25

Eleven-Minute Outline and Research 45

Fifty-five Minutes of Productive Writing 67

After the Draft 87

Resources... 97

A Little about Me

I have always been a writer. Before college I worked in the shipping department of a clothing distributor and was scribbling on the *Inspected by* scraps. After college, when driving a taxicab, I would take a few minutes between fares to write in my notebook.

In the corporate world, I worked as a technical writer, marketing writer, a software support specialist and in sales, and I always found a way to record something during the day—even if only at my lunch break. Writing is in my blood because I have ideas floating around my head almost every day and think some of them might be valuable to others.

I know that you have these flitting ideas as well, and I hope that you are or will begin to capture them. You might only record a phrase or word, but jot down enough to examine your thoughts later and decide whether they're worthy of working up into something more.

My vision for the world is that we live in a less stressful, less conflicted environment. I believe that when someone is busy creating, he or she has little time to criticize others or increase that discord. If writers are not happy with the world around them, they create their own. The world can be a better place if people find and practice their unique creative talents.

I left the corporate world just after the events of 9/11 shifted the business climate. I was caught in the wake of circumstances that shortly followed: The company where I worked had been recently acquired by another and that corporation used the event as a rationale to cut most of us working at their satellite location. I was devastated but decided the time had come to strike out on my own. I'd lived in the shadows of one corporate giant or government organization for most of my working life. This time I decided that if anyone would fire me, it would be me.

Using my skills as a technical and marketing writer, I ventured out starting a marketing business. My marketing business helped companies and solo entrepreneurs with customer acquisition through various writing services. My partners were all writers. We later added video. I had been a video hobbyist and brought on a professional who had worked in TV as a reporter and associate producer. All the while most of what we did for clients centered around one kind of writing or another.

The marketing landscape changed with the advent of social media. My company gained proficiency in social media platforms, and we learned to write blogs, work with search engine optimization (SEO) experts, produce web articles and write profiles among other skills necessary in this world of web-based advertising and sales.

I have been working on books throughout my whole career. In 1976 I published a book of poetry and worked through the entire publishing process from typesetting to printing and promotion with others who had these skills. I learned a great deal about the book creation business. I took the books out to bookstores and small shops, created marketing materials and developed the necessary sales skills. I have had a chance to see how all the pieces fit together and observe both the creative and business components in the writing game.

I also taught writing classes and mentored writing clients. This book is based on many of the lessons I have learned from those experiences and participants. As a former English teacher, before emigrating to the world of business, I had a good foundation in grammar and spelling as well as in composition and logic. I continue to take courses and learn about the art of writing, the craft of publishing both electronic (e-books) and traditional books, marketing and sales, and social psychology.

In this series, I intend to share as much of my knowledge and experience as I am able. This book, *Write Your Non-Fiction Book in 4 Weeks* is intended to help non-fiction writers produce their books in a short time by completing the first draft in four weeks or a little more. I hope you enjoy the book and the process.

Introduction

What is *Write Your Non-Fiction Book in 4 Weeks*?

This book is designed to help writers, especially those who are embarking on their first book, get into the flow of the writing process. I also wrote this book with the intention of helping those authors who have started books and left them incomplete.

Additionally, I hope to give authors who have already completed one or more books a few new ideas. Sometimes even seasoned authors face writer's block. Fortunately, most writers also have a thirst for knowledge and are continuously learning; so it is my hope this book can provide benefit.

Writing a book can be daunting. What if you could get started with just one minute a day for the first week? This is a guide about how to start and then keep going by completing exercises beginning with one minute a day for the first week and building to 55+ minutes the final week.

I have segmented the exercises into four chapters. Each of these takes you through a series of seven exercises for the week. One of the major difficulties in writing a book is the effort that is necessary. As a result, many people begin but do not finish. This book will help you start with small steps and encourage increased effort as you proceed through the four weeks.

Some of the exercises in chapters three and four may take longer than the allotted time. Do not be discouraged and, if you only have the allotted time, return to the exercise the next day. Some steps just take longer. Keep on moving even if your schedule slips. Be sure to follow all the steps. If you skip one, you may have to come back to it later when doing so will have a greater impact on writing or re-writing your book.

For example, if you have a significant amount of research to do, and you begin writing before you finish your research, you may have to re-write a portion of your manuscript in light of the research content you have found, or you may decide what you have written is not as relevant as you had first hoped and have to drop a section. I am reminded of a writer I know who had researched something historical on the web but during re-write could not verify the source. To be true to her audience, she had to delete multiple paragraphs and re-work around the original text after not including that information. This may happen even if you have done the research. You want to minimize the need to re-write.

What *Write Your Non-Fiction Book in 4 Weeks* is not

This is not a book about writing style, grammar or syntax rules. Many writers have already mastered these skills, and those topics are out of the scope of this book. Other books with that information are available. Some of my favorites are listed on my website, *Drewbecker.com(http://drewbecker.com/writing-resources/)* and in the final chapter, "Resources."

Conventions used in the book

I suggest you create a number of files as you work through the exercises in this book. The file names are written in all caps such as CHARACTER or WORD COUNT file. This is to help you immediately understand what file is being referenced.

I have also included a fictionalized author's experience with the process. We will follow her on her journey through the exercises. My intention is that watching her complete the four-week schedule will make the instructions a little more concrete.

Chapter 1
One-Minute Vision

The concept of *multiple creation* is as old as the hills. An early version was written by Wallace Wattles in his 1910 book, *The Science of Getting Rich*. He wrote:

> "Man is a thinking center, and can originate thought. All the forms that Man fashions with his hands must first exist in his thoughts; he cannot shape a thing until he has thought that thing."[1]

This concept was paraphrased by Stephen Covey when he wrote:

> "All things are created twice; first mentally; then physically. The key to creativity is to begin with the end in mind, with a vision and a blue print of the desired result."[2]

In order to produce something into the real world you must bring it into the world of your thoughts, and so it is with a book. Thus, the first exercise in creating your book or your chapter or section is to conceive it.

By dedicating one minute (or more) a day you can till the fertile ground for your manuscript, and in this chapter I will suggest how to do this. Before you can succeed, however, you must see your book not as a project but as a reality.

Where and when to do these exercises:

Find a quiet place where you will not be disturbed. Schedule the time and make arrangements not to be interrupted. Turn off your phone, close down all social media on your computer or shut down your computer and other devices. If you need to make notes, do so with paper and pen or pencil.

Some of the exercises must be done in your writing space; others can be done elsewhere.

By following this process, you will ingrain in your brain the idea of writing your book and also begin to see the end results. As these visions become clearer and more vivid, you will ready yourself to do the actual writing by using the processes described in the following chapters.

Until you *see yourself as a writer*, your task will be more difficult and you cannot expect others to see you as an author. Having others view you as an author is critical to promoting and selling your book once you have completed it.

The Exercises

Day 1 Visualization One

The first exercise can be done anywhere you can find solitude. Visualize your book. See it complete with the book cover, the binding and all the internal pages. Can you imagine it in the window of your favorite bookstore? Envision a stack of your books on a table or a spike on your Amazon dashboard indicating a massive number of e-book sales. Hold that picture in your mind. Make it real.

Make notes about any thoughts that come to mind. Print out your notes and title them FIRST VISUALIZATION file.

In addition to the visualization exercise, enlist support from family and/or friends for your writing project. During the next four weeks, you may find that you need someone else to help you keep your writing commitment. Find a person you can turn to at those times. Enlist a supporter or a network of people to create accountability. Some of you may want to hire a coach who will make your responsibility a scheduled event. When writing a book in a short period of time, you might want to be held accountable two or more times a week.

Day 2 Set Up Your Space

Set up your writing area. Unlike most of these exercises, this is a physical task. You will need to construct the right writing environment. Obviously, this is one of the steps that must be done in your writing area.

Place your favorite chair at a desk or, if necessary, at the dining room table. You will probably be working at a computer. You might also want to have a pencil or pen and tablet and sticky notes near at hand. I also like to make room for my favorite beverage (where it will not spill on any electronics or paper). This is important as many authors can attest to having spilled coffee, tea, water or something else on a keyboard or on notes.

NOTE: If you are going to write in a coffee house or outside your home or office, figure out what your set-up will look like. Will you have your phone and/or paper and pencil next to you?

You will want to get a physical file folder to keep together all your notes for your book as you go along. Put your notes from this exercise and the last one in your folder. Find a convenient location to keep the folder since you will be adding to it most days through the four weeks. If you will be working outside your home, secure a spot for the folder inside your computer case or in something else you will be carrying with you. Add any exercises later when you return home and can print them.

Make a few notes about what you have decided and label this page as WRITING ENVIRONMENT file. Print out this file and the one from yesterday, FIRST VISUALIZATION, and put them in your physical folder.

Day 3 Avatar

Today's exercise can be done anywhere you can find solitude. Sit still in your writing area or another serene place and create your avatar. An *avatar* is a representation of the reader who will buy your book; in fact, this is your ideal reader. Think quickly about who will enjoy or benefit from your book: Men or women? People working in a company, for themselves, or staying at home? What is his or her age? Give your avatar a name.

NOTE: Be sure you fully consider who your audience is before you write the book. For a fuller understanding, see Day 3 in Chapter 5.

You will want to write down some ideas after you think about this exercise. Have a pencil or pen and paper handy, but **do not begin writing** until you have finished building the image in your mind.

Entitle this exercise AVATAR and add the notes to your physical folder.

Day 4 Book Launch

Visualize your book launch.

This exercise can be done anywhere you can be alone and undisturbed. If you will be producing a physical book, will you have an in-person event? Who will you invite? Where will you hold the event?

If you are releasing an e-book, will you have a web event? Will you announce it through social media? Will you use Facebook, LinkedIn, Instagram? Will you create a video or set up a Google Hangout or Skype virtual book tour? Who will you invite, and what time will you arrange it?

Remember, the more detailed your visualization is, the better your results.

Make notes from your exercise and add them to your physical folder. Title your notes BOOK LAUNCH.

Day 5 The Interview

Visualize being interviewed on the radio, a podcast or on TV.

This exercise can be done anywhere you can find solitude. Will you be on a radio broadcast? Who could you contact locally to be on a show? On whose podcast will you be the guest? Whose podcasts do you listen to and could you reach out to be a guest? What TV station will be the first to want to interview this famous or soon-to-be famous author?

Once again, make notes and add to your folder. Title this file as INTERVIEW.

Day 6 The Book Signing

Visualize signing copies or, if you are writing an e-book, emailing a signed cover to your readers.

This exercise can be done anywhere you can find solitude. At your live event, envision yourself sitting at a table with a hefty stack of books at your side and another box under the table. A line has formed in front of you and you are in conversation with fans. You pause and then look down to autograph a copy with a special note to your most ardent supporter.

You may visualize the dashboard on your Amazon bookshelf, where you see the digital copies fly into cyberspace as readers purchase more and more of your book.

Day 7 Rest

You have spent a week with these exercises to help you build the solid vision and the motivation necessary to keep your writing going. Take a day away from the exercises and see if any other ideas emerge. If so, you may want to record them.

Meet Our Non-fiction Author, Jill

Let's examine how this process might work with a non-fiction writer. We will follow Jill through all the one-minute processes.

Jill is a professional woman who works 50 hours a week. She is married and has children who are in elementary school. Jill has multiple responsibilities competing for her time; so writing a book can be a challenge.

Jill is five foot three and has long brunette hair. She likes to read fiction and non-fiction as well as magazines about business and more personal matters. She is in the PTA and also attends other functions where her children are involved. She is married to Pat a CEO of a high-tech company and they have two daughters. She likes ballroom dancing, tennis and watching movies. She was brought up in a middle-class family and was always the most ambitious of her siblings. She liked English and history best in school and penned a few creative writing stories while in high school but didn't show them to anyone. Her interest in writing only occurred after she was in her corporate position.

Jill decides the best way for her to accomplish her writing task is to set a schedule in the evening when her partner is there to keep the kids occupied. She will slip away into another room to do this work. One way to help her family understand what she is doing is to tell her kids that she has to do homework and that is why she is going into her office.

If her partner, Pat, is not available, Jill may have to complete her exercises after the kids go to bed.

Let's see how she does her *One-Minute Vision* exercises.

Day 1

Jill imagines that her book about how to balance family life and work life is a 6" by 9" (width by height) paperback [229mm X 152mm- height by width] and a Kindle edition that can be read on a laptop or a phone. The book has a green cover with a picture of a woman facing in two directions. Her book title, *Both Ways*, with a working subtitle, *Living a Complete Life,* stands out in fire-engine red as does her name as the author. The paperback has a half-inch thick spine, and she sees it standing up in front of her. She picks it up and thumbs through the pages. Her Kindle version has the same front cover graphic and she imagines it on the Kindle Amazon site and the Barnes and Noble website.

Day 2

Jill once again visualizes her book in front of her in all its shining glory. Next she clears her desk of other projects and turns on her laptop. To the left is her phone, which she will only use as a resource in case she needs to check something while she is writing. She sets the sound to mute and places it on a surface where the vibration will be absorbed. During her writing sessions, her cell remains off or muted so as not to distract her. To the right, Jill has a spiral notebook to keep notes that may occur to her but are not necessarily related to the section she is writing. She has adjusted her chair to be comfortable but not too much so. Her beverage is also set on a coaster to the right.

Day 3

First Jill envisions her book title and subtitle and then settles into her writing area with all her tools and her drink in hand. Jill begins to define her avatar. As introduced earlier, an avatar is a representation of the reader whom you want to buy your book. Jill sees a female in her early 30s, say 32, who has a family with three children and works during the day in a professional capacity. Jill names her Diana. She imagines a technical manager in a multi-national corporation. Diana has a six-figure salary and has attained her position by working long hours. Her significant other has flexible hours; so child-rearing responsibilities can be shared.

Day 4

Jill begins thinking about her web launch. She can imagine contacting all her Facebook friends to tell them about the publication of her book. She decides to offer her book at a significant discount for the first week. She realizes that before doing that, she will need to get pre-final versions out to get recommendations from other writers she respects including one who has a national reputation.

She might even set up a Skype or a Google Hangout video call so that she can read from chapter one. She will have to connect with her friend who does webinars to figure out exactly how to make this happen. Her writing in that first chapter about how to have a family and professional life will include a paragraph that gives a valuable tip that viewers can implement immediately. "Oh," she thinks, "I need to let my LinkedIn contacts know as well, and I will post in Google Plus and also snap a picture of myself with the book cover for Instagram. What other platforms will work for me?" she asks herself.

Day 5

Jill scours the web and looks for podcasts featuring authors. She finds some large, nationally-recognized shows but also seeks some others that are newer and have fewer listeners. She thinks about whom she knows at a local TV or radio station and considers which friends and acquaintances may know someone who could help her get an interview. She also investigates local newspapers and magazines. She can imagine herself on local radio talking with the host and discussing how her book can help other professional women.

Day 6

Standing in front of an audience, Jill discusses the advantages of living "both ways." She expounds on the importance of personal achievement as well as the satisfaction of being a great mother to her children. At the back of the room, her assistant is setting out books for sale for her to sign at the break. Confident about the sales of her e-book followed by the published paperback, she feels self-assured as she speaks.

Day 7

Today Jill spends the whole day with her family. If stray thoughts arise related to the book, she will make a quick note, but she will not follow up with writing anything of length.

Notes

Notes

Chapter 2
Four-Minute Foundations

Congratulations on finishing the *One-Minute Vision* exercises. You now have some momentum and can move forward in your preparations.

Each one of the next set of exercises takes four (4) minutes. These practices will help build a foundation for your book. Both strategy and tactics are necessary to complete this week's exercises. Let's be sure we have a common understanding of these words. In this book *strategy* refers to a plan or method to achieve goals, and *tactics* are the techniques and actions used to get that done.

Exercises

Day 1 Purpose

What is the purpose of your book? Think of purpose as the intention of the book, its reason to be. Determining the purpose is essential to creating the bones for your book since that structure will help you attain your book goals.

Consider both your purpose for the reader and your own intention as the author. The reader purpose is the foundation for why he or she would want to read your book. Your author purpose centers around why you are writing the book.

To discern your purpose, consider these questions.

Reader Purpose:

- What will this book do for the reader?
- Will the reader learn a new skill or process?
- Will he or she get an overview of a new technique from the author?
- Will readers be educated so they can begin new ventures, make money or improve health?
- Will he or she learn a new theory and how to apply it?
- Is this a self-help book that will guide the readers through a series of exercises to enhance their lives?
- Will you entertain your readers?
- Will the readers change their attitudes or get a better understanding of themselves and others?

Writer Purpose:

- How do I want to interest the audience while reading?
- How do I want to engage the reader after reading the book?
- Do I want to tell my story?
- Do I want to promote another book?
- Do I want to be recognized as an authority in my field?
- Do I want to promote a workshop or seminar?
- How do I enable the reader to communicate with me?
- How do I encourage the reader to spread the word about my book?

Create your PURPOSE page and record your answers to both sets of questions.

Understanding the dual purposes of the book is critical to determine structure, how you will write it, what you will include and what you will exclude.

Print out a sheet of paper with PURPOSE as the title at the top and add notes about your purpose. Add this file to your physical folder.

Day 2 Introduction to Perspective/Person

Another important choice that writers have to make is about perspective. Who is speaking in the book determines how it is written. There are three dimensions to consider: Person, Number of Viewpoints and Voice.

Your choices about person, number of viewpoints and voice over the next three days will be determined by how you want to present your material. If you prefer a more subjective view, tell it from the writer's vantage point. You might want to be more objective and act as an outsider looking on as a narrator. Another option is to tell it from multiple character viewpoints. Once you have determined this, you can begin making choices about person, number and voice.

NOTE: One of the best books to make choices for these three exercises is Characters and Viewpoint[3] by Orson Scott Card. Although this book is aimed primarily at fiction writers, its knowledge can be applied to nonfiction as well.

Person

The easiest way to work through perspective is to select the *person* first. Person is the term many of us learned in English class. It refers to whether the speaker is *I*, *you* or *he/she*.

First Person

Memoirs are written in the first person as are other non-fiction books that relay a personal story about the author. This is a favorite format for books that use the personal story to motivate including self-help and healing books. First person is also used in some business application books such as business improvement and education about specific skills. This perspective may be mixed with others as will be noted in the next few paragraphs.

Second Person

Many non-fiction books are created to explain a process. These are often written in the second person and include instructions. Recipe books are written this way along with instructional guides that take the reader through step-by-step processes. Some first person books will also include a second person perspective when explaining how to accomplish tasks. In fact, a significant number of non-fiction books switch between these points of view depending on the type of material being presented.

Third Person

One convention used by some writers is to tell the story of a main character so the reader can learn as the character does. Readers discover the information the author wants to share by "riding along." This requires the author to tell a compelling story while conveying the information.

A few non-fiction business books like *Raving Fans* by Ken Blanchard and Sheldon Bowles employ this technique. The reader learns about customer service with the Area Manager as he follows his Fairy Godmother (a man, no less) to see how to accomplish tasks. The book uses this clever technique to help the reader understand through storytelling.

You notice I include a narrative at the end of each chapter to show how someone might apply the exercises in a story. I shift to the third person in these sections. I introduced the concept in my introduction; so readers are prepared for the shift in viewpoint.

Enter your person perspective on the page or pages as PERSPECTIVE 1 file. Add this information to your physical folder.

Day 3 Number of Viewpoints

The next consideration when selecting a perspective is the *number of viewpoints*.

This refers to how many people are telling the story. Do you talk directly to your audience, or is there a main character who speaks for the author? Do you employ both? Do you have one or more characters telling the story?

Non-fiction books usually stick to one person or may move between the first and second in order to have the immediacy of the first person and informality of the second. As a writer you may find yourself also shifting between the two of these as you write. In some cases you might use all three. Decide what works for you.

Enter your decision and label the page or pages as PERSPECTIVE 2. Add this information to your physical folder.

Day 4 Voice

Once you know how many viewpoints you are going to present and whose perspective(s) those are, you are ready for the next decision. You must create the *voice* for each viewpoint. Voice refers to the language and world view of the writer, narrator and/or character(s).

Voice is important in non-fiction. Although you do not have to delineate between characters—a critical technique in fiction—a standardized voice is critical. As you write you may want to be casual, somewhat formal or very formal depending on your subject matter and your experience with that topic. Choose one voice and stay with it unless you have more than one character and/or a narrator (who could be the author).

A casual tone works well when the book is presented in a light-hearted way, but when an MD discusses family genetics, a more formal tone would be more fitting. A formal tone often denotes an expert in the field who is presenting a deeply researched topic. Think of the difference between an article in *People Magazine* and *The New York Times*. The first is chatty while the second is direct in language and style.

Make your voice fit your material. If the voice is not consistent with the presentation, you may lose the reader.

Fill in the page or pages labeled PERSPECTIVE 3. Add this information to your physical folder.

Day 5 Structure

Let me talk about the concept of *structure*. Many writers like to work in an organic way and resist the idea of structure, or it is at least foreign to them. I understand this too well and have shied away from any structured approach to my own writing until recently. My "just flow with it" process, however, has created a number of half-written books in both fiction and non-fiction.

Structure has to be viewed as a guideline rather than a strict, binding form that holds the book and the author in a stranglehold. If the original map does not get the author to the destination he or she is headed towards, it is necessary to "re-calculate" as my GPS says. This is a great metaphor for writing: Feel free to revise your direction as you go; however, do not go back and rewrite until you finish your first draft.

Many business books include the *what* and *why* but not the *how* as a strategy to compel the reader to contact the author to "do it for them." Although a standard practice for many years, readers are more savvy today and expect some of the *how*. As a result, many current authors of business books will include enough to get the reader started. How do they encourage readers to use their services? Even though many or all of the steps may be included, they demonstrate that using the author's help will save time and money. Many readers want the work done for them and will seek help from the author even when the steps have been laid out for them.

Non-fiction books often use one of the following structures or templates:

- Problem and solution
- Problem, solution, implementation
- Present situation, possible changes, outcomes

Problem and Solution

In the problem section or sections, writers often introduce themselves and explain their experience with the challenge. That challenge is described in depth and may be segmented into finer points which can be addressed in the solution sections. The solution section may include processes or suggestions to meet the challenge.

Problem, Solution, Implementation

This structure is similar to that used in the *Problem and Solution* template and adds an implementation section. Instead of describing the solution in one part, a general remedy to the issue is presented. In the final section, a specific path and detailed processes are described. This portion of the book often includes tactics to achieve the strategies.

Present Situation, Possible Changes, Outcomes

The third structure begins with the Present Situation and often includes a history of how that has evolved. Possible Changes suggests a number of actions or a complete plan (strategy) with steps that could be pursued (tactics). The author might compare different plans and actions to each other. In the Outcomes section, the writer will suggest the best course of action and predict how the solution will help the reader.

With any of these writing tactics, the writer may share stories throughout the sections to help the reader understand how the author and/or others have approached the challenge to improve their businesses, relationships or lives.

Label the page or pages with your notes as STRUCTURE. Add this information to your physical folder.

Day 6 Reconsider in Light of Purpose

You have made critical decisions this week about your book. Now it is time to re-read your purpose and think about how the different aspects of perspective and structure fit into what you have chosen. Look at each of your choices and determine if they are aligned with both types of book purposes. Have the intentions of the book changed as you investigated these other elements?

If all these factors are still congruent, you are finished. However, if the purposes have changed, make modifications, or if some of these elements do not move your purpose forward, modify the misaligned elements to match your aims.

This alignment will become more crucial as the book continues. For those of you who have hit a wall in writing, check your material and see if these elements line up well.

Go back to your PURPOSE file and make any additions or changes. Re-print the file and add it to the physical folder. The title will still be PURPOSE.

Day 7 Rest

Spending a week with these exercises has helped you build a solid foundation to begin your writing. Get away from your computer and reward yourself. Again, see if any other ideas emerge. If so, you may want to record them quickly. Be sure to get some rest.

Returning to Jill

Let's catch up with Jill and see how she works through her *Four-Minute Foundations* exercises. Jill has now imagined her book about balancing family and work, established her writing environment, created her avatar, and visualized her launch, interview and signing party. The exercises this week build the foundation for writing the book.

Day 1

Jill sits at her desk and begins thinking about her aim in writing the book and the purpose the book will serve for readers. Both of these ideas need to be completed *before* the writing begins in order to set the boundaries for what the book will cover.

Stealing minutes from her early morning before others in her household are awake, she begins the process. She has not articulated what the purpose for the book might be for her readers—at least not significantly.

She has a conversation with herself. The conversation turns into a dialog with her alter ego.

"I know that I want to write the book to help other women like me to balance home and work life," Jill begins.

"How can I do that?" her alter ego inquires. "I need to make this clearer for myself."

Jill replies, "What I need to figure is how my strategies and tactics helped me to develop a balanced lifestyle. These are what I have to offer to my audience. I need to determine what to do and how to do it. After my readers have finished the book, they should have some ways to examine their own lives to see how much balance they already have and then use some of my ideas to improve their lives. Okay, that's a little clearer."

Alter ego responds, "All right, since you seem to have a better idea what your readers will get from the book, what do you hope to get from writing it? Do you want to be a *New York Times* Number One Best Seller? Do you want to boost your reputation as a life-balance coach? Is this a hobby or just a gift for friends?"

"Good question. I've thought about what I want my audience to get but haven't actually considered what I want from the book. I can see I will need to know this to keep me writing. I would like to become a well-known coach in my market, and I hope friends and other readers would buy this.

"I'm glad I had this conversation since it has helped me to see where I am going. Thanks, alter ego. Now I will print out these purposes and pin them above my desk," Jill concludes.

Day 2

Jill next tackles the first of the perspective exercises. She finds this easy because for her there will be only one perspective, *hers* as the writer. She leans back in her chair and thinks, "That was easy."

However, as she is congratulating herself, she realizes there may be more to this than she first thought. If she is going to use examples, will she tell all those stories from her point of view? Probably not. So how many other "characters" will she have in her book? Which ones will tell their own stories and which stories will she tell? Now she realizes that she will be using more than one perspective.

So Jill now knows that she may shift points of view. Even though most of the story will be told in the first person, she will have at least one other point of view.

Day 3

Now Jill must consider the number of viewpoints. She looks back at yesterday's exercise and sees that she will definitely write most of the book from the first person.

She also knows that sometimes she will speak directly to the readers and use the second person. This will be especially useful when giving directions for how to accomplish tactics she includes in the book. Finally, she acknowledges that she might tell some of the stories from the point of view of some of the people in the examples.

Jill will have to stay conscious of which point of view she is using and be sure her audience can distinguish among them. These multiple points of view need to be clear in her mind so they are evident to her readers.

Day 4

Jill feels she is on a roll as she approaches day four and will decide on a voice for the book. She feels confident about how the book will unfold, knowing she will write most of it in the first person. However, she might also shift as she adds accounts from other characters in examples. She will be vigilant to differentiate these voices unless the narrator tells their stories.

Jill knows that because her audience is mostly busy women who have family and work obligations (see Avatar exercise, Week one, day three), she will have to write in a quick, easy-to-read style. Her audience is already scrambling to get everything done on two or more fronts. She decides to write in a succinct, casual voice.

Using this style should appeal to her audience. Her sentences will be short and the book will be focused and a fast read. If she doesn't follow these rules for voice, her potential readers may not pick up the book at all. The voice could be similar to magazine articles in *Vogue*, *Cosmopolitan* or *Forbes*, and although casual, it will have a sense of authority to project her business side.

Satisfied with her considerations for the day, she closes her computer and heads in to have a cup of coffee before finishing her household duties and heading out to her job. The thought floats through her mind that someday with the book written she might be able to create her own schedule with ultimate flexibility.

Day 5

Now that Jill knows about some of the elements necessary for her book, she thinks about how it might be structured. Her friend Cathy is a writing coach and has helped a number of other authors put their books together. She offered to help if Jill gets stuck when Jill first began to write.

Jill calls and finds that Cathy can meet her for lunch that day. After working through the morning, Jill hurries to a sandwich shop nearby to meet her friend and coach. After they have ordered, Jill shares what she has completed.

During lunch Cathy suggests a variation on the *Problem and Solution* structure. They decide the best structure is to write a section on problems and one on solutions with examples. A third part will follow with exercises to help the reader. The final portion will suggest resources to help the readers if they need further information and will include a description of Jill's program.

Jill happily picks up the check and heads back to her office. She is excited and can feel that this book is really going to happen.

Day 6

With all the details in mind from this week, Jill revisits the notes she took about purpose. All her information about the purpose for the reader can stay the same. She is on track after completing the other exercises for the week.

However, her own author's goals have expanded as she has gone through the week. When she thinks of herself at the end of this project, she would like to use the book to promote workshops across the country so she can impact a large number of women and be able to make a living selling her book and workshops. She has realized that an exciting aspect of the publication is that it can help launch her career through workshops and speaking. She understands that she will be able to work for herself and control her schedule, leading to new opportunities to keep her life in balance.

"I just might be creating my second book as I go through this writing process and the book catapults my new career," she tells herself.

Day 7

Jill spends the day with her family. She is successful in not even thinking about her book and separating her author life from her family life, one of the tactics she will include in the book. She enjoys cooking and playing with her children and ending the night sharing a glass of wine with Pat.

Notes

Drew Becker

Notes

Chapter 3
Eleven-Minute Outline and Research

As described in the last chapter, a certain amount of structure can help with your writing. In this series of 11-minute exercises, you will frame the book. As a author you have to have an end in mind while writing. We discussed purpose in the first chapter, which is a good guidepost for non-fiction, and you can benefit from filling in some of the stops along the road to direct the writing and stay on course.

In addition, you might need to research to gather the information needed to complete your manuscript. This might entail gathering supporting information for your premise or stories to back up your points.

Exercises

Day 1 Outline

Even if the outline begins with no more detail than the chapter titles, this process can help you. Outlining your non-fiction book is crucial to successful writing.

The first step to building your outline is to consider your book's overall structure. The type of book you write will dictate the best organizational choice to present your book to your audience. Look back at your purpose to help determine this. I mentioned some options for a few different types of organization when discussing structure in Chapter 4 Day 5. Review your STRUCTURE file.

Here are some possibilities for outline organization based on the type of book you are writing:

Personal Development

Books about personal development and health and healing often begin with a personal story.

This is followed by a description of the challenges and proposed solutions, which are often described in step-by-step processes with a checklists or schedules for implementation.

Business

Business books use other templates. Depending on the

business domain, these can differ. For the novice writer, the basic approach is the easiest. The basic template has three elements:

- The Problem (a description of the issue, history of treatments, etc.)
- The Solution
- Implementation

The *Problem* can contain a description of the situation that needs to be examined, a brief discussion of what has been done previously and other processes and stakeholders who might be affected.

The *Solution* section could include entries for a strategy to solve the challenge and a variety of possible tactics to pursue.

The *Implementation* might list processes and caveats for executing the solution in an organization or company.

Self-Help Health and Healing

A self-help book about health might use the *Problem-Solution* template. Like in a personal development book, this could begin with the author's story including a brief view of the issue. The next section of the book would define that problem in more detail and might add others' experience when they met the same challenges. The final section would cover a solution or multiple remedies proposed by the author. Variations of the *Problem-Solution* template are used in many self-help books.

Using one of these templates or your own variation of that model, build your outline so you can begin working on the different chapters as you go. Create a more detailed outline under each section and then you can look at the full structure of your book.

Record your notes and construct your OUTLINE file. Be sure to make a hard copy of your work and place it in your physical folder.

Day 2 Determining Your Research Needs for the Market

Research is often the major component in non-fiction even if the author is providing all the content. You will want to research to be sure your book is more than a rehash of what has already been written. As the author, you have a unique view of the material, but that may not be enough to create value for your readers. How can you add to what has already been published?

Your research begins with what has been written and then investigates your unique information for the book. If a significant amount of research is necessary, you might do this in parallel with your writing. For most writers it is more efficient to do the majority of the research first. Then they can avoid altering the writing already done.

Research is somewhat easier today with the internet, but be cautious of what you read online. One of the advantages of looking at published materials is that the publisher should have fact-checked what is written. Blogs and other materials on the web may be accurate, but chances are that these resources have not been checked and verified. Finding a secondary source is always a good idea. You may want to use a third verified source if you have any doubts.

Day 3 Continue Research of the Marketplace

You started yesterday by setting the scope for your research. Today continue with the research to prepare to write the book and market it.

To refine the research on your market, go to a physical bookstore and to an online bookstore like Amazon or Barnes & Noble and look at the categories for your type of non-fiction book. Under what category could your book be classified if it were on the site or in a bookstore? In your local bookstore read the back covers, and you will see what categories publishers have chosen for their books. Online, that information is printed below the book information in what is referred to as metadata.

The figure below is from *Interviewing Quick Guide: The Art and Craft*, my first book in the Writers Blocks series. You can see the metadata categories and ranking when it was first released.

Enhanced Typesetting: Not Enabled
Amazon Best Sellers Rank: #4,986 Paid in Kindle Store (See Top 100 Paid in Kindle Store)
   #1 in Books > Business & Money > Skills > **Business Writing**
   #1 in Books > Computers & Technology > Graphics & Design > **Electronic Documents**
   #1 in Kindle Store > Kindle eBooks > Business & Money > Skills > **Business Writing**

You can see that the categories it was registered for were:

- Business & Money > Skills > Business Writing

- Computers & Technology > Graphics & Design > Electronic Documents

- Kindle eBooks > Business & Money > Skills > Business Writing

These were determined after research.

Now delve into what books are in your categories. Books are listed with three categories as seen above. Check out each of the categories for books similar to yours.

Look at the best-sellers and see how they are written. You can read the beginning of many online books with the "Look Inside" feature on Amazon. Discover how bestselling authors begin their books and what voice they are using to address their audience. You don't want to copy their style, but it is a good idea to identify what people are buying.

To conclude this task, read reviews of the books you are researching. What do readers like and dislike about other books in your category?

Special Considerations:

Categories are important for any type of book but probably most important for non-fiction, especially if the author is using the book to promote other products and services. Remember who this audience is so that you can focus efforts to *mine* those prospects.

Save your work as AUDIENCE RESEARCH, print out what you have discovered and place it in your physical folder.

Days 4 & 5 Determine Your Research and Begin

Once you have your list of the research topics required, begin your search. This may take more than one session; so dedicate the fourth and fifth day to this task. You will want to complete the majority of your research before moving on.

NOTE: If you are not able to complete this in the allotted time, set a schedule for doing your research. You may have to complete this work before writing; so other exercises may be delayed.

Research can cover a lot of ground depending on the topic of your book. You will want to consider at least four aspects:

- Background
- New information
- Information supplemental to your knowledge
- Fact checking your information

Background

Think of this part of your research as a dual approach. Examine both areas: what exists and what you will add.

First, what has already been written on your topic? You will need to survey the field to see what has already been published. Of course, even if many authors have worked with your topic, you can bring something new. Consider your experiences, new data and your insights that haven't been written about previously. In some cases, after research you may find you don't need other sources. Your ideas may be adequate without outside corroboration.

Secondly, on what will you base your information, and what sources are you going to cite? This material might include case studies and references to previous information including radio and television interviews, periodicals, newspaper articles, blog posts, e-books and traditional books. Collect this data in notes and be sure to give proper credit to other authors as you go to avoid having to search for the citation when you reference this material later.

New Information

Have you scoured enough sources to be sure you are offering something new? If needed, go back to researching and use the most up-to-date information. Releasing a book with the newest knowledge is sure to increase its value to the reader. This is one reason authors offer revisions of their books.

Supplemental Information

What else do you need to know? Complete your task by taking care of any other research you may not have done to this point. This might include looking at the news to see that nothing else has happened since you began or contacting that final illusive source.

Fact Checking

Perform fact-checking on what you think you know. Remember if you have doubts about any of the material you are referencing, validate from somewhere else. Some sources may not verify their information, especially these days with blogs and open source information portals.

Wikipedia can be an author's best friend and worst nightmare. While some information is checked on a daily basis, not all entries can be verified in a timely manner and some are not checked at all. The decision to confirm entries is mostly voluntary. If I find something in Wikipedia, I look for the primary article or media where it originated. After validating the authenticity, I use it unless I still have reservations. If I am not totally comfortable, I look for an additional reliable source to assure me that the information is correct or do not include the research.

When writing a blog recently, I was looking for the average number of times per day children hear the word "no." One source stated that a one-year-old hears it over 400 times a day (146,000 times a year) *[http://answers.google.com/answers/threadview?id=516517]*. Other studies report significantly different numbers, saying that number is 40,000 times by the age of five *[http://home.znet.com/mrdoug/no.html]*. I quoted both sources and pointed out the discrepancy, but then explained whichever source was correct, the results were still devastating for a child's ego.

All these aspects of research may take more than the two sessions; so you may want to return to it after you are finished with the Day 6 exercise. Take a short break, then resume your work.

Most authors continue research during the writing phase. Do your best to be content with what you have completed and realize you may need to do more of this work next week.

Print out the information you have collected, and save it in the CONTENT RESEARCH file. Place that in your physical file folder for the book.

Day 6 Filling in and Revising the Outline

With your research completed or nearly completed, you are ready to revisit your outline. Retrieve that from your files.

What new items for your outline have you added during research? How do these fit into the structure of the book? Revising now is much easier than later when you are deep in the writing stage.

Updating at this point is an important step many writers skip, then regret during the writing and editing phases. By moving on without updating, they may have to restructure after writing. This process can be tedious and includes determining what has been written previously and scouring the work to find references that may have changed.

If you move a part of the book to rearrange it before other sections, you need to review all your references in that portion, because you may have written assuming the reader already knows something that has not yet been presented. By organizing before writing, you can save yourself headaches and time during revision and editing.

Revise your OUTLINE file. Print it to use when you begin your writing next week. Place the file back in the folder.

Day 7 Rest and Review

You have had a busy week completing all these exercises. If you still have work to do, you may have to slip the schedule or take more time out of your relaxation day. Even if you do cut into this time, be sure to get some rest and walk away from the project at some point before beginning the final set of exercises.

Returning to Jill's Writing

Day 1 Outline

Jill is ready to write her outline. She goes back to the set of notes she took when she and Cathy met for lunch. Using her notes, she sees natural divisions and determines that she will begin with the section about the author. She commits her six sections to paper:

- About the Author
- Introduction
- Problem
- Solution with Examples
- Exercises
- Resources

Under the About the Author section, she determines there are five stages of work she has experienced. Each of these will become a sub-section:

1. Early corporate
2. Marriage and corporate
3. Leaving corporate to have children
4. Rejoining corporate
5. Exit corporate for her own business

Jill will return to the *Introduction* once she has written the book. Looking at the whole manuscript she will be able to introduce the reader to each of the sections.

Seeing that the first two sections of the book are taking shape helps her to dive down deeper in the outline. She will detail each item in the next section, *Problem*.

The *Problem* section follows the stages she outlined in the *About the Author* section and adds more details. Here is her first draft of that part of her outline:

Her Early Corporate outline looks like this:

III. Problem

    A. Early Corporate

        1. Dating and work

            a. Scheduling week nights

            b. Scheduling weekends

        2. Seeing Friends

        3. Seeing Family

        4. Return to School

She will now detail items for the Seeing Friends, Seeing Family and Returning to School entries as she did for Dating and Work.

The *Solutions* section will mirror the *Problem* section and include examples. Jill defers her decision as to which solutions will have accompanying examples. She has three or four scenarios to include and a few more in mind. She adds an entry for all of these to the outline.

The *Exercises* section will include a few activities she uses with current clients and others she will research. As long as there is a placeholder for this part of the outline, she is satisfied.

The *Resource* section will be completed later. Jill has not determined how she will organize entries in this section; so a placeholder for this is adequate.

As she is finishing her outline it occurs to her that she does not have a section describing her program. She fills in the outline for this to include her program description:

VI. The Balance Program

    A. Introduction

    B. The four foundations

        1. Foundation 1

        2. Foundation 2

        3. Foundation 3

        4. Foundation 4

    C. Program Content

    D. Registration and special offer

Her revised high-level outline will look like this:

    I. About the author

    II. Problem

    III. Solution with examples

    IV. Exercises

    V. Resources

    VI. The Program

Day 2 Determining Your Research Needs for the Market

Jill has a double dose of market research because she is going to publish her work as an e-book and a paperback. Jill goes to her favorite bookstore to look at titles. She seeks out the manager who knows her, and they talk for a few minutes. The manager directs her to the *Women's Issues* shelves to do her research.

There she peruses all the books on the shelf and pulls down a few to skim. Jill thumbs through all of them, looking at the table of contents and scanning whatever catches her eye in terms of subject matter she will cover. She smiles often because she sees that a number of the topics she is going to cover are not in any of the books. Of course, some of her topics are.

That night at home, after the children are in bed, she turns on her computer and begins the same process on the Amazon and

Barnes and Noble websites. Instead of skimming, she reads from the "Look Inside" section of a number of books. Unlike the dozen or so books in the book store, over 100 titles come up. She begins scanning the top sellers. After going through another 10, she turns the computer off and spends some time with her mate before going to sleep.

NOTE: Jill decides to return to this work by spending extra time on the weekend. She looks ahead at the rest of the exercises for the week and realizes she can get some of them done on days four and five. Anything she does not complete, she will move to the weekend.

Day 3 Continue Research of the Marketplace

The next day she returns to her favorite bookstore to do more research to determine where the book will fit. It might be placed in more than one location in another bookstore, but she returns to *Women's Issues*.

Jill finds 14 books that have work-life balance themes. She makes notes of the categories printed on the back of these books. Eleven of the books have categories on the back covers. Of these, six list *Self Help* as one of the categories. Five list *Women's Issues* and four identify as *Personal Growth*.

That evening Jill does the same research on Amazon and Barnes and Noble. She scours the top 100 books in her categories. She finds this topic in Kindle books in two categories:

- Kindle Store: Kindle eBooks: Business & Money: Business Life: Time Management
- Kindle Store: Kindle eBooks: Nonfiction: Business & Investing: Business Life: Time Management.

The number of books about work-life balance total less than 800, and there are under 20 about work-life balance for women. She hones in on and reviews the books that are specific to her topic.

She realizes that if there are this number of books on time management there is a market for that topic.

NOTE:

Jill again decides to spend more time over the weekend or push out her schedule if she is not satisfied with her progress at the end of day 5.

Days 4 and 5 Determine Your Research and Begin

Jill's first task on day 4 is to review what she has learned from at the bookstore and on the internet. She finds she has a good grasp of what's out there, and she enjoys the fact she can read more online previews. She spends the rest of the time collecting information from the course she has developed and finding additional resources and making note of them. She also reads the reviews.

On Day 5 she gathers more information and plans to complete this task over the weekend. However, she gets engrossed in the project and spends over an hour pulling together the majority of what she will need for the book.

Day 6 Filling in and Revising the Outline

Jill is tired at work today and considers skipping the exercise tonight. In spite of her resistance, she retrieves her outline again and reviews it in terms of the information she has been gathering. She is able to enhance several sections she had previously started.

These small revisions are easy after the intense work all week. She goes back downstairs to share wine with her mate and discusses how good she feels about completing the week.

Day 7 Rest and Review

Determined to stay on schedule Jill talks to her family and asks for some extra time to "finish her homework." They agree and she carves out three additional hours to work. Due to this "overtime," she does not review and decides she will do that during lunch the next day for a few minutes, then will continue by completing the final week of exercises.

Notes

Notes

Chapter 4
Fifty-five Minutes of Productive Writing

This chapter is for those who have completed the first three weeks and have a good handle on vision, foundations and the outline and have finished most of their research. You are now ready to begin composing your book. Now is the time to focus on the writing itself. You may also find that you have to return to your research during this week.

NOTE: How many of you have already begun writing? I know that a number of you got the fever sometime during the vision week, but I hope you have held off doing so. Working though the sequence presented in this book is the easiest way to get your book completed. However, if you have started writing already, don't go back over what you have written in terms of all the exercises to this point. RESIST! You need to finish your first draft before doing any editing.

I have found that writing is a curious thing. Once I get on a roll, I want to continue non-stop without sleeping or eating. Obviously that isn't healthy or sustainable. Be sure not to blow all your energy in your early writing sessions and burn out halfway through the race. Finishing a book (even in four weeks) is usually a marathon—rarely a sprint.

In each session write for 55 minutes straight without interruption. Please control your urges to answer calls, look at social media on your computer or phone, or open other applications on your computer. Gift yourself this period of time and schedule it the same way you would an important meeting.

Even with the best intentions to focus you can still be undermined. If that happens, break up your writing time into four 15-minute segments. However, you will require over an hour since each time you are interrupted and begin again, you will need a few minutes to get back into the groove.

Handling Interruptions

I am often interrupted during my writing time. When I am ready for a session, I go to that mental space I have dedicated to the task. I have learned to overcome the guilt I used to feel based on the thoughts that I should be doing something else. With external and internal blocks erased, I focus and write for the time block or beyond. (Remember not to burn out!)

Whether you are interrupted or not, remember that this is a commitment to yourself. If you want to get this work done, you have to keep going. In addition, *please* avoid blaming and chastising yourself for the interruptions. Let it go. Simply return to your writing. I know writers who have internal discussions about how they have let themselves down instead of dedicating that time to writing. So if you are interrupted, get back to it as soon as possible.

Another problem that writers have is that other ideas pop into their minds while writing. Don't allow yourself to get sidetracked by additional thoughts or tasks other than the writing. Let these things go for as long as it takes to get this first draft written. If an idea for something else in the book floats into your consciousness, make a note on a piece of paper and get back to the work at hand.

Depending on the length of your book and how quickly you write, you may need more than 55 minutes a day to complete your draft. You are in charge of your schedule. Only you know how committed you are to finishing your book.

One way to determine how much time you need is to estimate the number of words you will require based on page count. If you are writing an 80-page book, your word count will be approximately 20,000 words. Each page has approximately 250 words. For an 80-page book, you will have to write just over 13 pages a day or 3300 words. If you can write 10 pages (2500 words) a day for eight days, you will be done.

Another thing for novices to remember is that you will move faster the more you write. I did not feel like my writing emerged until after I had completed my first 250-page manuscript. I will probably never go back and edit and publish that book, but it helped me to quicken my pace and to improve my writing.

Completing a longer book will take more time, of course. If the number of pages is large, plan to spend more hours a day or more weeks to finish your draft.

One other strategy is to use a program to dictate and then convert speech to text. Copy the results into your book file(s). Most of us speak much faster than we type; therefore, this can save time as well. Be aware that using one of these programs makes it likely that you will have to make a large number of corrections to the text. Although continuously improving, this type of software rarely translates accurately. Do not polish the results, simply modify them enough to reflect your spoken thoughts.

Exercises
Day 1 Writing

Begin filling in your outline. I use a tool, [Easy Writer Pro, which is free at the time of this writing](). This software only works on PCs, but an equivalent, which may or may not have a cost associated with it, is likely available for other platforms. This software allows me to set up my chapters from my outline and select the chapter that I want to write. I can return to a saved chapter and add to it, and I can also add new chapters as I write. I have added the link to get *Easy Writer Pro* in the beginning and the end of the book.

Some writers prefer to use word processing software such as *Microsoft Word*™ or an equivalent, and that also works. The challenge may be to keep track of all the chapters and then, if necessary, to maintain moved chapters in order.

It is often easier not to start with the introduction but to jump right into the first chapter. Introductions are often written last. Grab your printed outline and start writing that first chapter on your computer.

Write for the full 55 minutes if possible. If you are interrupted, you will want to go back and use the strategy presented earlier in this chapter.

At the end of each writing session, I perform a word count. This entails exporting in *Easy Writer Pro* and then using *Word* to perform the task.

Do your word count only after completing your session; otherwise, you might break your concentration with this activity. I create a file to keep track of my word count per day after the session. The current version of word keeps track of this in the lower left of the window and when working in Word, I keep myself from looking during my writing period. Afterward, I use *Excel*™ and simply enter the dates and the word count. In the third column, I divide the word count by 250 to get an approximate page count. This serves to help me ascertain how well I did with my projected number of pages if the book is printer in 8/12 x 11.

NOTE: If you decide to take a day or two or the weekend to do a marathon writing session, you may be able to move more quickly toward your goal. Remember to get some rest though so you are fresh when you write again. In a marathon session, I get up, stretch and walk around every hour or two. Be sure to save before you leave your writing. If you get tired or feel your productivity declining, take a break. When you come back, if you feel burned out, let it go for the day.

Write non-stop as best you can. Do not worry too much about spelling as long as you can understand what you are saying. Although you may be tempted to re-read and re-write as you go, this is a bad idea; don't do it.

I tell you this because before I finished my first non-fiction book (and fiction book for that matter), I kept reworking the writing. I spent so much energy trying to get the wording perfect that I often lost track of the ideas I was presenting and my train of thought. After revising, I would come back and feel like I was starting over again. I was successful in completing my draft only when I wrote straight through without worrying about spelling, grammar and punctuation.

Your book may begin with a brief section in which you, the author, introduce yourself and explain why you are qualified to write the book. This chapter, like the introduction also may be a difficult starting point.

Again, my advice is to go to the first chapter that deals with your subject matter. This is often the easiest place to start. I find the best method during a session is to stay with one chapter until you have finished writing for the day. If you complete one chapter during your session, then move on to another. You do not have to write your chapters in order, but be aware that any references you make in that part of the book must be based on material in a previous section. I will discuss moving parts of your book later in this chapter.

As you write, please save your work **often**. Save more often than you think you need to, because the one time you don't you might lose your work. No matter what software I have used, I have lost writing because I did not save enough.

Once you have written for 55 minutes or longer and saved your work, you might want to reward yourself by doing a word count. As I indicated at the end of each writing session I do a word count by exporting from *Easy Writer Pro* to *Word* and performing a word count.

Days 2-6 Writing

Return to your writing refreshed. Remember to follow these suggestions:

- Take a few moments to switch gears and move into your writing mode.
- Keep in mind why you are writing and who your avatar is.
- You might read the end of what you wrote yesterday but do not take too much time to read that whole chapter.
- ***Do Not*** begin editing because you will eat up today's writing time doing so.
- As soon as you can, begin writing again.

In most cases I pick up where I left off, but sometimes I feel inspired to write a different chapter. Follow your instincts about where you write each session. As I said, in most cases I return to where I left off the day before.

Once you have the first day of writing behind you, the following days should get progressively easier. With all your past research in mind, continue your writing, moving along as quickly as you can. Sometimes you may need to do some minimal revision as you go. You might add a paragraph before one that is already written or perhaps rearrange things a bit. This is fine; just keep writing. If you are going to edit, remember to keep revisions to a minimum, but **I advise you not to do this.**

Continue working on the chapter you have started or write in a different one. You may need to stop writing to do research along the way. Try to finish a section of the chapter or the chapter itself before you change tasks. Hopefully you have completed most of your research before you write, but sometimes more will be needed.

Researching uses a different part of the brain from writing. We automatically do these switches in everyday life without being conscious of them. You need to be aware that this switch will take you out of your writing mode. This is necessary in many cases and is not in itself detrimental.

When the research is completed and you are ready to return to the writing, realize this shift in how you use your brain affects you. Some writers shift back and forth between research and writing as they go. This is acceptable if it works for you. If you find it hard to return to writing after doing more research, you may want to pause for a few minutes, take some deep breaths, get something to drink and/or eat and then re-enter your writing mode.

Be careful when moving material in your book. This advice seems logical and simple, but you can create a mismatch if you do not consider all the ramifications. You may find that certain information in your book works better if it is moved to another location. This could be paragraphs, parts of a chapter, or even full chapters. The *Easy Writer Pro* software enables you to relocate chapters with ease. However, when you do move words, paragraphs or chapters, be aware of any references you made in the moved material or to that material elsewhere in the book.

For example, if you write that step four follows completing step three and you have changed step three to step five, the reference will be mislabeled. Another challenge might be if in step three you refer to the previous step (step two) but this step is now step five; your reference is incorrect.

Although I do not recommend that you edit as you are working on the writing, it is sometimes necessary to correct these kinds of things. Only make changes if they are necessary to get through the draft.

If you must skip around among the chapters you are writing, try to stay within the same section of the book. To keep things rolling, it is generally easier to write the book sequentially. However, in some cases it may be more efficient to jump between chapters to connect certain concepts. I will discuss an example of this in Jill's story later.

You are at a critical state with your writing at this point. If you have not yet finished, stay focused and keep writing. The last 5-10% of the book can be the most difficult, but you need to keep working since you are so close. Find someone to encourage you. Call on your support person or team and ask for help.

Write for your 55 minutes or longer, saving as you go, and at the completion perform your word count again. Record your numbers and evaluate how you are doing.

Day 7

Many of you will have a first draft written. If so, take a well-deserved break. Print the draft out and put it away. Do not open the files on your computer or look at the hard copy for a few days. Go out and celebrate your completion.

If you have not finished, keep writing to complete the first draft. Although this is designated a rest day, it is the last day of your writing so make the last push and write through this session. If necessary, add days to complete the draft but try to keep your session short enough so you continue to the finish line. When adding days be sure to keep your day of rest. As I stated before, the last 5-10% of the writing can be the most difficult, but you need to keep working since you are so close. When you finish, be sure to reward yourself.

Jill's Writing

Day 1

Jill begins her week of writing by completing the page count exercise and determining that she will have to write 11 pages per day to complete the book in a week. She has timed herself and realizes that if she is focused she can write 10 pages in an hour. She will either have to extend her writing time or extend the number of days she will be writing. She decides to extend her writing time and set the goal of finishing the book in the allotted week.

She dives into the content of her book, beginning her writing the third chapter describing the problem. Following her outline, she describes how the life balance challenge first emerged as she took her first corporate job after graduation with her undergraduate degree. She describes her first job and how it impacted her personal life and how difficult it was to find time for friends and family, especially after she enrolled in a Master's program.

She details how she lost balance of her life after returning to school. She often had to choose between time with her family and time with her friends. Jill had a hectic schedule at that time in her life and rarely slept more than four hours a night. She was willing to make this sacrifice to get her degree and advance her career. Her social life was also delayed and when she had time, she went out with friends and was determined not to get involved in a serious relationship.

She goes on to write about meeting her mate. She realized she wanted to date occasionally, but she found that most prospects she met were either too busy or not serious enough for her. Then she met Pat who also had a busy schedule and things changed. They found a way to steal minutes from their busy days to form their relationship and later were engaged and married.

This leads Jill into writing about the marriage and corporate challenges she faced. She describes the many difficulties she and Pat had due to their extremely busy schedules.

She then writes about leaving corporate to have children, returning to the corporate world and finally leaving to build her own business. Before she knows it, her chapter is nearly finished.

She looks at the clock and is surprised she has been writing for an hour-and-a-half. She saves her work and does her word count for the session and enters the number in her WORD COUNT file. With a feeling of success on this first day of writing, she heads back downstairs and spends a few minutes with Pat before turning in for the night.

Day 2

Jill picks up with the next section, *Solutions*. She describes how she worked to resolve the balance issue when she first entered the corporate world. She follows the description with a couple of examples of what she did during those years. She also adds stories from others which she has noted in her outline.

Once completed, she moves to her years in corporate after marriage. Before beginning, however, she realizes she is still thinking about the early corporate years. Jill opens the file for the *Exercises* chapter and, accessing her research, constructs three different exercises that will help her audience to attain balance in their lives.

She returns to the *Solutions* chapter and writes about life-work balance as a married woman in a corporation. She adds her examples and closes the chapter. She opens the *Exercises* chapter and enters the exercises that relate to the Marriage and Corporate section.

Jill closes the laptop, happy with her progress. She exports and enters her word count into her WORD COUNT file. She joins her family downstairs. She checks her watch and sees that she has written for 80 minutes.

Day 3

Jill opens her files and realizes that she needs to outline exercises for the remaining three phases of her work life. She spends her writing time building those exercises to be used for the rest of the week. Although she is tempted to write out the full exercises, she forces herself to list bullets for each. Once she has finished, she can go back and add more text to each exercise. She looks at her watch and realizes she has been working for two hours.

After doing her word count and entering it into her WORD COUNT file, she joins Pat downstairs. She apologizes for writing so long and explains why it had happened. Pat is understanding and supportive of her writing and smiles, giving her an affectionate hug. She realizes how important it is to have this support during her writing process.

Day 4

This session is productive. With her research from yesterday, she is able to complete both the "Leaving Corporate to Have Children" and "Rejoining Corporate" phases of the *Solutions* chapter and flushes out these parts of the *Exercises* chapter. She completes her writing ritual with the export and word count activities and is done in 40 minutes. Pat is surprised to see her so early.

Day 5

Jill opens the files on her laptop and works first in *Solutions* on the "Exit Corporate" phase. This is a complex part of each of those chapters, and the *Solutions* chapter ends up taking more time than expected. Since this is the most recent phase, she has a harder time culling examples from her life. Then she writes for a while in the *Exercises* chapter.

Once those chapters are finished, she moves to the *Resources* chapter, where most of the work is formatting and arranging the items since she marked resources as she did her research. She first decides to organize the resources to match the chapters and within each of these groupings to alphabetize the items.

She finally does small revisions in the "About the Author" and composes the "Introduction" section. Each of these is easy since she already has a summary of her experiences in her first visit to the chapter and has written the book. Therefore, she knows exactly what she wants to include in the introduction.

Day 6

Jill's sixth writing day is dedicated to explaining her program. Using her outline, she writes the introduction and a summary of each of the *Four Foundations*. Once the summaries are completed, she fills in more information about each of these. Describing the content of the program comes next. Here she does strong copy writing to spur interest in the program. To complete the chapter, she adds information about registration and makes a special offer for readers.

After a 70-minute session, she saves, exports and records her final word count on the WORD COUNT file. She had written about 17,000 words, a good number for a small book. This would translate into around 45 8 ½ x 11 pages. If the book is in 6" x 9" (229 x 152 mm) format, it would be longer.

Jill prints her manuscript and puts it into a folder. She places the folder in a drawer, and, with a wonderful smile on her face, goes to bed.

Day 7

Jill and Pat send the kids to one of the grandparents and they make a day of it. They walk in the park, have a light lunch, take in a movie and afterwards have an elaborate dinner, then drive home to spend some intimate time together with a bottle of Jill's favorite wine, Cabernet Sauvignon.

Notes

Drew Becker

Notes

Chapter 5
After the Draft

Congratulations! Now that you have finished writing your draft, put it away for one to seven days and then read it from a fresh perspective—as a reader, not the writer. Next, you will want to complete three tasks before sending your manuscript to a publisher or publishing it yourself:

- Self-edit and send it to someone else to edit.
- Format as an e-book or for traditional printing or submit to a publisher with cover letter.
- Plan and execute publicity.

I easily could and might write books about each of these topics but in this chapter I will briefly describe each of them.

Edit

Finishing that first draft is a bit of a sprint. Once you have finished the draft, put it away for at least a day. When you pull the manuscript out of the drawer, approach it as if someone else wrote it. You might want to read it four times before getting someone else to look at it.

Editing your own material can be difficult and is rarely as much fun as writing the book. You need to do a number of edits to save time and money before submitting to a professional editor. Editors with whom I have worked ask for a sample to evaluate in order to ascertain how much time and work will be needed; from that they create a price estimate.

When you are ready to work on your manuscript, read it for:

- Continuity
- Logic
- Impact
- Grammar, spelling and punctuation

First, read for continuity. When a team makes a movie, a script supervisor plays a vital role. During filming, that person watches what is happening to be sure that characters are wearing the same clothes from one session to another, that the props are placed in the same place, that hair styles are consistent. When you read for continuity, you want to be sure your ideas and presentation are consistent. Be sure that all the concepts follow naturally and that you have consistency in elements like tense, person and voice.

Read for logic. Does the book make sense? If you have processes, re-read, and if possible execute them to make sure they are complete and can be followed. Read and test as if you were seeing this for the first time from a reader's perspective. Have you arranged the chapters in the easiest order to understand?

Are there instructions or descriptions in later chapters that rely on information presented in an earlier chapter? Check to determine if any are missing, because this can happen if you moved chapters.

Read for impact. When you edit the third time, be sure you are presenting your information with the greatest impact. Check each sentence to consider whether you made the best word choices and expressed these in the best order. Look to see that each sentence carries the reader to the next. Each chapter ending should make the reader want to move to the next one with curiosity and anticipation for what follows.

Most non-fiction books encourage the reader to take some action. Have you provided adequate motivation to prompt what you want the reader to do? Re-write if the answer to any of these questions is "no."

Read for grammar and spelling. Finally, read to check for grammar, punctuation and spelling errors. Do not rely solely on your word processor's spell check and grammar checks. Look for errors on your own. Confirm that you have only one space between sentences.

Many writers don't remember all the punctuation rules, especially those about commas. If you are one of those, get an online reference or a book that describes the use and rules of punctuation. Check your spelling carefully. Make sure you have written complete sentences (unless you are sure that a sentence fragment conveys all of your meaning). Readers may be critical of your writing if you use incomplete sentences even if you like writing this way.

When you do the final self-edit, be aware that the human mind fills in the blanks or missing information. Nowhere is this more dangerous for us writers than when we re-read our own work. Our brains tend to see what we think we wrote. Check all these editing steps, especially the last one, with that in mind.

Format/Submission for Self-Published or Small Press Works

The format for your book is dictated by the platform and the publisher or the printer. There are significant differences between e-book and traditional or print book printing.

The Internal Pages e-book

If you are publishing an e-book, you will need to find what file formats are accepted by Amazon, Barnes and Noble or any other online publisher. Amazon will accept *Microsoft Word* unfiltered *html* files or a *.mobi* file. If your book has complex internal formatting, you may need to get help from an outside source who can program those difficult sections.

The Internal Pages print

For print book publishing you will have to determine the size of your book and number of pages as well as other specifications including fonts, margins, gutters and more. Will you have perfect binding (a spine with printing on it) or another type of binding? Will the book be a paperback or hardback?

Formatting the Inside of Your Book

You can learn to format your text and graphics for the inside of your book yourself or hire someone to format for you. E-books are easy enough to build unless there is complex formatting. In that case, you might need to enlist the help of a programmer. Print books, on the other hand, take more expertise, and you may want to get help from someone who can build your book in a professional program like *Adobe InDesign*™.

I formatted my first e-books and am happy that I did. However, there was a learning curve *with Easy Writer Pro* although nowhere as lengthy a one as with a professional product like *InDesign*.

Cover Creation

They say you can't judge a book by the cover, but in today's competitive world you need a cover that will attract the attention of your potential readers. My first non-fiction book had a self-designed cover. I'm a writer, not a designer, and my original home-made cover reflected that. To start, I needed to get the book out quickly and did not allow time or budget to have a cover done for me. I have since had a professional graphic designer create a cover for this entire series. My books now look as professional on the outside as they are on the inside.

The Cover

You will need graphics for your book cover.

For an e-book this is usually a high-resolution *.jpg*. Different print publishers and printers will ask for a *.pdf* file or a *.jpg* with specific margins, gutters and pre-sets for a *.pdf*. You will be required to deliver a different file for the cover.

Submitting Your Book for Traditional Publishing

When you submit your book to a traditional publisher, they will take care of the formatting for the print and e-book editions. You must present your writing in their suggested format for them to look at it. Preparing work for a traditional publisher is beyond the scope of this book, but you begin by finding out what the publisher wants and writing a compelling cover letter. One source for learning this information about publishers is *Writers Market,* which comes out with a new edition annually.

Publicity

Begin letting people know about your book while you are still writing it. Once your book is published, doing publicity is critical. You must publicize your book so you can earn money and/or enhance your reputation. For authors who are introverts—and many of us work in solitude and tend to be at least inwardly motivated—this can be a challenging step. *No one can sell a book like the author.* Even with a traditional publisher, unless you are a well-known author, you will not get much help publicizing your book. If you opt in to paid-for publicity, which some independent publishers offer, you will still be the best salesperson for your book.

After I self-published a poetry book, I went to all the local bookstores and asked them to carry my book. Only a few—mostly independent stores—agreed to stock it for me. They took it on consignment and it was my responsibility to check back weekly or monthly to collect any profits from sales. Today you can sell online through Amazon which wasn't a possibility at that time. Nevertheless, just uploading your e-book or putting your book up for sale is not enough. You will need to be the best salesperson for your own work. Consider doing readings at bookstores and libraries.

You can use social media to sell, but most authors whom I know begin by selling their own books person to person. If it catches on, Amazon can help as well as other organizations. Try the local newspaper and magazines. You may want to take out an ad in one of those publications.

Remember when we visualized the interview in the first week? Now is the time to set up a session with local radio and television stations. You may also want to arrange an interview with a host who has an internet platform such as Blogspot or iHeartRadio.

Get creative. Think of where your readers are and find a means to connect with them. What Meetup.com groups in your area would be interested in having you speak? Are there other organizations you could approach who would be interested in your topic? Remember to build your marketing around your avatar.

Allow your readers to interact with you. Develop a relationship with the reader so you can create raving fans.

Enjoy your author status and have fun with your book. You have put forth a great effort and I wish you all the rewards you can think of for yourself.

Notes

Notes

Chapter 6
Resources

Footnotes:

[1] Wallace Wattles (1910). *The Science of Getting Rich* Holyoke, Mass: Elizabeth Towne Company.

[2] Stephen Covey (2004). *The 7 Habits of Highly Effective People* New York: Simon & Shuster.

[3] Orson Scott Card (1988) *Characters and Viewpoint* Cincinnati: Writer's Digest Books.

These are the files mentioned in this book:

- FIRST VISUALIZATION file
- WRITING ENVIRONMENT file
- AVATAR file
- BOOK LAUNCH file
- INTERVIEW file
- PURPOSE file
- AUDIENCE RESEARCH file
- CONTENT RESEARCH file
- WORD COUNT file

BONUS: Email the author for templates for these files at Drew@RealizationPress.com.

Here are a few resources:

> *Characters and Viewpoint* by Orson Scott Card
>
> *Elements of Style* by William Strunk
>
> *Rules for Writers* by Diana Hacker
>
> *A Manual of Style* on University of Chicago Press
>
> *Writers Market*

Easy Writer Pro software - available at no cost at the time of the book production

www.easywriterpro.com

Need help to stay on course?

See the Writing Accountability Program:
drewbecker.com/accountability

Acknowledgements

Although writing is a solo endeavor, no book project is done alone. There has been a team working behind the scenes to help me complete this.

I would like to thank a number of people who have made this book possible. There are more folks than I can list, but here are a few.

First and foremost, thanks to my wife, Diana Henderson, who gifted me time to write this book and later did the final editing. You are an angel.

A few years ago Pat Howlett, a great friend and supporter helped me discover my path as a publisher and as a trainer for Easy Writer Pro software. His influence and encouragement has been key in the production of this book and my publishing company.

After I released the first book in this series, *Interviewing Quick Guide: The Art and the Craft* (an e-book), Jennifer Davis of Rockbrand Creative offered to look at the cover. We have worked subsequently to design a professional cover for the series.

My friend Michelle Hill of Winning Proof with whom I team with on multiple projects, gave the book a view before I sent it to my editor, and we became accountability partners to be sure we get our writing done as well as our respective businesses.

Kristen Joy challenged me a few years ago to write my first non-fiction book. She is now one of my mentors. Through my association with her and her writing and publishing community, I have been privy to valuable resources and extensive advice.

Other mentors assist me in ways that are critical to my success. These include Martin Brossman for social media, Bill Davis for business advice and Divya Parekh for coaching.

Omar McCallop is a co-producer for the Triangle Book & Writer Conference which is slated to be an annual event in the Raleigh, North Carolina area.

I have been attending the Apex Small Business Network for a few years, and their support for my first book and patience as I have talked about this book is greatly appreciated.

A myriad of other people too numerous to be named have encouraged me to write this book.

I also must credit my writing clients, who helped me refine the concepts presented in the book.

Oh, and finally, thanks to our sometimes patient parrots who spent more time alone since I dedicated myself to finishing this project.

www.ingramcontent.com/pod-product-compliance
Lightning Source LLC
Chambersburg PA
CBHW071743080526
44588CB00013B/2140